THE ULTIMATE GUIDE TO HUNTING™

INSIDER TIPS FOR HUNTING VARMINT

XINA M. UHL AND
JUDY MONROE PETERSON

rosen publishing's
rosen central®

New York

Published in 2019 by The Rosen Publishing Group, Inc.
29 East 21st Street, New York, NY 10010

First Edition

Library of Congress Cataloging-in-Publication Data

Names: Uhl, Xina M., author. | Peterson, Judy Monroe, author.
Title: Insider tips for hunting varmint / Xina M. Uhl and Judy Monroe Peterson.
Description: New York : Rosen Central, 2019. | Series: The ultimate guide to hunting | Includes bibliographical references and index. | Audience: Grades 5–8.
Identifiers: LCCN 2017048354| ISBN 9781508181866 (library bound) | ISBN 9781508181873 (pbk.)
Subjects: LCSH: Varmint hunting—Juvenile literature.
Classification: LCC SK336 .U35 2019 | DDC 799.2/5—dc23
LC record available at https://lccn.loc.gov/2017048354

Manufactured in the United States of America

CONTENTS

INTRODUCTION

Another word for vermin is "varmint," a troublesome wild animal. Varmints can be different animals—usually small mammals such as raccoons, opossums, coyotes, bobcats, and prairie dogs. They qualify as nuisances for a number of reasons. Perhaps they kill or endanger farm animals like chickens, sheep, or livestock. They may damage pastures, eat crops, or destroy crops altogether. They may carry diseases and overpopulate an area. Perhaps they become invasive species that displace the resident species. Raccoons, bobcats, and coyotes are big enough to kill or maim family pets and farm animals alike, while prairie dogs and gophers can dig numerous holes and tunnels in the ground that may not only be unsightly but also become tripping hazards. When animals are injured, they require veterinary care, which can be costly. More costly still are the deaths of valuable domesticated animals. Whatever the reason varmints are nuisances to humans, hunting them is considered pest control designed to protect property, the lives of domesticated animals, and in some cases, small children.

Hunting varmints can be a more environmentally friendly method of pest control than poisons such as rodenticides. These poisons can head up the food chain, affecting larger predators. For instance, anticoagulant rodenticide poisons remain in the varmint after they are dead. Mountain lions, bears, and birds of prey like hawks or eagles can eat the dead varmint and then suffer the deadly effects of the poison in the varmint. A California National Parks Service study found that 92 percent of the area's mountain lions were exposed to these poisons, which often cause poor health and lingering deaths.

Gopher holes can be frustrating. The 1980 comedy *Caddyshack*, starring Bill Murray, features a scene in which Bill Murray's character goes to war with a mischievous gopher.

Varmint hunters are able to practice and improve their shooting skills year round since many varmints, such as coyotes, can be hunted during every month of the year. The definition of a varmint varies by region, so it is necessary to understand what a varmint is and whether or not that animal is regulated by local wildlife department laws.

It may surprise some hunters to find out that certain varmints may not be attempted by beginning hunters. Hunters may require high-powered scopes and rifles and other special and sometimes expensive equipment. Certain varmint hunters must travel long distances to reach an animal's habitat. Prairie dogs, for example, inhabit states in the West like New Mexico. Beginning hunters need not dismay, though. With a little time and effort, they can locate experienced varmint hunt-

Raccoons, like the one in this photo, can look cute, but they are one of the primary carriers of the rabies virus in the United States.

ers to introduce them to the sport and mentor them as they become proficient in it.

Varmint hunting provides the opportunity to refine hunters' shooting skills year round. The quarry is a challenge because they are often active primarily at night and are adept at hiding and escaping from pursuers. Some varmints, like bobcats, have claws and teeth as means of defense, making them sources of potential danger to people or their dogs. Some hunters sell their raccoon, coyote, and bobcat furs. Raccoon and opossum meat is enjoyed by hunters, but that is not the case with coyotes, bobcats, and prairie dogs. Instead, the reward of hunting varmints is usually in the thrill of the hunt and the satisfaction of ridding an area of pests that can cause significant damage.

CHAPTER ONE

BASICS ABOUT THE HUNT

Varmints can go by different names depending on your state and region, including nuisance animals, vermin, and pests. Hunters need to understand local laws and regulations concerning varmint-hunting season, including which animals can be hunted, using which methods.

WHAT MAKES A VARMINT

Varmints are generally small game that are considered a nuisance or pest because of their overpopulation or their negative impact on people. The excess population makes these small game animals a problem for people, particularly farmers and ranchers. In the United States, animals that are often considered varmints include raccoons, opossums, coyotes, bobcats, and prairie dogs.

Raccoons and opossums can destroy crops and damage property. Coyotes and bobcats can injure or kill valuable farm animals and pets. People and pets, such as dogs and cats, can die from rabies. This disease can be transmitted by the bite of an infected raccoon, opossum, or coyote. Prairie dogs are a significant reservoir of bubonic plague, which can then infect other wildlife and pet animals. Bubonic plague is an infection transmitted by the bite of an infected flea. Prairie dogs can harbor infected fleas. To transmit the disease, the flea must bite a person. The plague can be cured in its early stages if treated by medications known as antibiotics. Without treatment, the plague is usually deadly. Prairie dogs can overpopulate a ranch or farm and cause damage to livestock and crops.

FOLLOWING THE LAWS

No legal definition of a varmint exists in the United States. Each state determines which big or small game animals are consid-

The name "opossum" comes from an Algonquin Indian name that means "white dog."

ered varmints. The definition of a varmint can change from state to state. States' departments of natural resources publish the current hunting regulations on their websites and in free booklets. Varmints may be open game on private land for year-round hunting in one state but may have a controlled hunting season in an adjoining state. In addition, sometimes hunting regulations for varmints vary within areas of a state.

States and the federal government allow liberal hunting seasons and generous or unlimited bag limits for animals that, from time to time, are considered pesky varmints. The hunting of varmints is a management tool used by states' departments of natural resources to control excess or nuisance wild animal

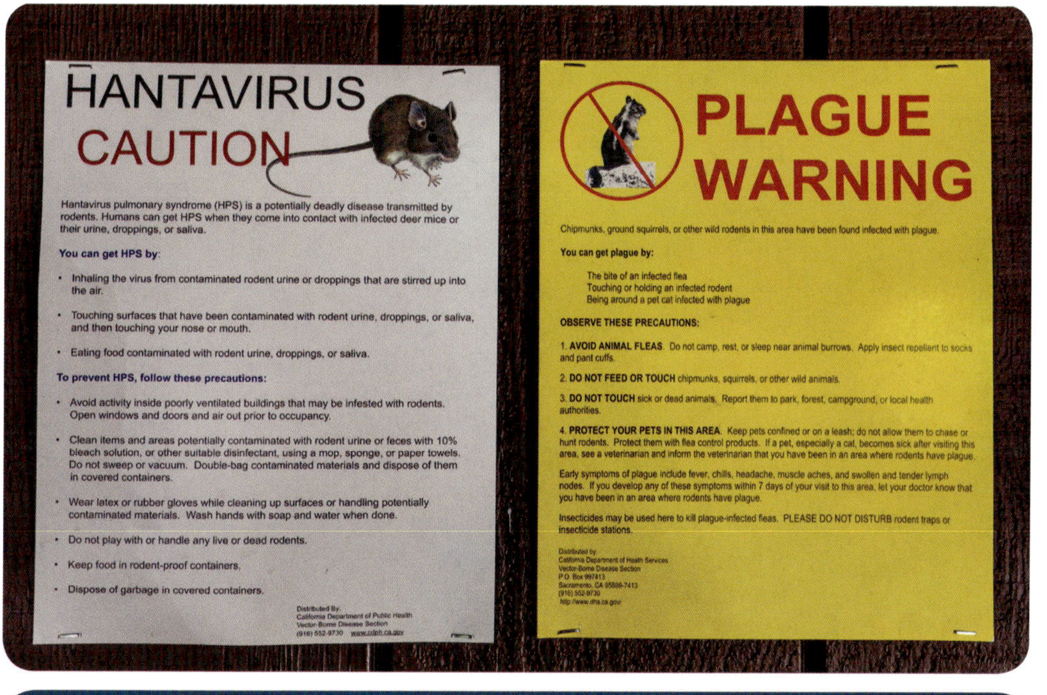

There are areas in states such as California and Arizona where some animals are infected with bubonic plague or hantavirus, both serious illnesses that can be transmitted to humans.

In the mythology of many Native Americans, the coyote is known as a trickster who provided humans with fire and daylight.

populations. In many states, varmints are both hunted and trapped. Sometimes a state's regulations specify that people can hunt and trap a particular, combined number of animals per season.

Some states classify small game, such as raccoons, coyotes, and bobcats, as furbearing animals. During the hunting seasons, these states may allow furbearers to be trapped. Whether hunted or trapped, this classification of varmint as a furbearer has a maximum per season bag limit regardless of the method of animal harvest.

PROFILE OF COYOTES AND BOBCATS

Coyotes are considered varmints because they kill farm livestock and young wildlife. In addition, coyotes kill pet dogs and cats in suburban and rural areas. A population of coyotes can increase rapidly in an area. When this happens, the animals become a nuisance to pet owners and area farmers and ranchers. Although the coyote has been intensively harvested in parts of the United States, its population has increased across the country. Many states have broad hunting seasons for this animal. Some may have no bag limits. The season for coyotes varies from state to state and can be during the summer, fall, or winter months.

The bobcat is one of three types of wildcat found in North America. It is the most common wildcat on the continent. Bobcats will kill and eat a variety of small animals and birds. Because this predator does not discriminate between wild animals and valuable farm animals, they can be a nuisance to farmers and ranchers. The season for bobcats is usually during the fall and winter. States vary but tend to set the season with snowy months to allow hunters to track these animals.

PROFILE OF PRAIRIE DOGS

Several types of prairie dogs are found throughout the prairie and flat, grassland areas of the western United States. These wild rodents live in large groups called villages. Sometimes five hundred or more prairie dogs live in one small area, in homes that they make by burrowing deep into the ground. If the villages are in a farmer's or rancher's pasture, the prairie dogs are considered a nuisance. They can eat and destroy farm crops and also create deep burrows in the ground, into which livestock can trip, fall, and break a leg. In addition, the large prairie dog populations are hosts to fleas and viruses that can cause plague or flea reactions in livestock or pets.

In some states, prairie dogs are considered a nuisance varmint and can be harvested year round on private land. The season in that same state, on public land, may vary. In South Dakota, for instance, prairie dogs cannot be hunted in the spring. The hunting of these animals is not permitted in some public lands in the state. Few hunters pursue prairie dogs because hunting them requires much time, travel, and expense. People who

Prairie dogs have become pampered pets in Japan since the 1990s. Young animals can be tamed but adult prairie dogs can be vicious.

hunt these small rodents enjoy the challenge of extremely long, difficult shooting at small, moving animals.

PROFILE OF RACCOONS AND OPOSSUMS

Raccoons are widely considered to be varmint. They can cause serious damage to farmland and livestock. Two favorite foods of raccoons are corn and eggs. Farmers who grow corn or raise poultry, such as chickens, turkeys, ducks, or geese, may find that raccoons are a serious threat to their livelihood. Many states have generous hunting seasons for this animal, from summer or fall through winter. The bag limit varies depending on the state and season. In Arkansas, for example, the bag limit is two per day in the fall, and there is no bag limit from mid-November through the end of March.

Opossums are a troublesome animal for farmers. They are a nuisance because they may live in and under farm buildings and destroy crops. Like raccoons, they will eat the eggs of a farmer's poultry. Farmers who have a large number of opossums on their property are usually willing to have hunters eliminate their varmint population. Many states have liberal hunting seasons for this animal. For example, in Wisconsin, no season limits, bag limits, size limits, or possession limits exist for opossums.

REQUIREMENTS FOR VARMINT HUNTERS

Varmint hunters must know the hunting laws for the state. The laws include bag limits, legal hours, license requirements, seasons, any special regulations, and allowable gear such as

HUNTERS AND PUBLIC LANDS

Hunters show good ethics when they are respectful of other people and their land. They must not trespass or hunt on private land without the permission of the landowner. It is also illegal to trespass. National and state forests are public lands that may require special permits for access to hunt. It is important to read the federal and state regulations to determine how hunting access can be obtained. Public land is owned by all citizens. Some public lands are wildlife management refuges, in which hunting is generally not allowed. Varmint hunters on public property have a duty to treat the land with care. Whether on private or public land, hunters should know how to avoid damaging prairies and other fragile environments. For example, they should drive vehicles without harming the land or water in the area. People should always clean up after they are done hunting. It is good manners to pick up other people's litter. Some people are afraid of weapons or are uncomfortable seeing harvested animals. Hunters should not openly display their guns or harvest. They should also properly dispose of any offal (organs) and spent carcasses (animal parts that are not used).

headlights. Some states, for example, require a night permit to hunt. Hunters are responsible for knowing the type of firearms and archery equipment and when—the time of day or night—they can be used. People can get free hunting law booklets from local hunting license dealers, from the state's department of natural resources office, or on the department's website.

The shooting of animals other than during the specified time of day or season is called poaching. It is illegal to poach, meaning it is a crime. When they are caught, poachers can receive legal penalties, including time in jail and large monetary fines. Their guns and archery equipment will be taken away. They also may lose any vehicles used in the illegal hunt.

Every varmint hunter is responsible for making each hunt as safe as possible. Hunters must know how their rifles and other equipment work and how to shoot their firearms and archery safely around other hunters, animals, and on private or public property. Sometimes other people, such as wild berry pickers, campers, or hikers, may be using the land at the same time as a varmint hunter.

The flexibility for hunters to shoot at small, fast, and hard-to-hit wild animals during many months of the year provides excellent shooting practice for the hunter. Varmint hunting often requires long-distance shooting, sometimes a quarter mile (402 meters) or more. Many free resources on varmint hunting are available at public libraries, including books, magazines, and educational videos. Local shotgun or rifle clubs, gun dealers, and sporting clubs have experienced varmint hunters who are willing to teach beginning shooters. Wildlife managers, or biologists, with the state's department of natural resources and farm or ranch organizations often can provide advice and information for locating nuisance or overpopulated varmints to hunt.

CHAPTER TWO

CHARACTERISTICS OF VARMINTS

A successful hunt involves correctly identifying the habitat and behavior of varmints in order to predict their locations and actions. Predictable actions are habits connected with essential behaviors like breeding, finding shelter and food, communicating with one another, and attacking or defending themselves against predators. Animals live and move in specific territories.

ABOUT THE COYOTE

Coyotes, also called brush wolves, will eat nearly anything, including insects, crops such as corn, and fruits such as watermelon and berries. They hunt at night and most often prey on small animals. For example, they will hunt rabbits, gophers, prairie dogs, birds, and rodents such as mice, voles, and squirrels. They devour other animals, too, such as fish, frogs, and toads. Sometimes they kill goats, calves, lambs, fawns, and pet cats and dogs. When they are unable to find fresh food, coyotes eat carrion. They fear and typically stay away from people.

Along with its wide-ranging diet, the coyote can adapt to a variety of environments. It inhabits much of North America and continues to extend its range. West of the Mississippi River, the western coyote roams the open prairies, mountains, deserts, and some waterways. On the eastern side of the river, the habitat of the coyote is hardwood forests, brushy areas, and farmland.

Nimble and quick, coyotes can run up to 40 miles per hour (64 kilometers per hour) but usually average 25 to 30 miles per hour (40–50 km/h). They are highly intelligent and have excellent senses of vision and smell. These private, sneaky animals have an uncanny ability to move around without being seen or heard. Coyotes have pointed ears, a narrow muzzle (mouth, nose, and jaw), and grayish-brown fur with white chest hair. They measure about 48 inches (1.2 m) in length, including their 11- to 16-inch

The number of bobcats worldwide has nearly tripled since the 1980s. These animals may number more than 3.5 million.

(28–41 cm) tail. They stand about 24 inches (0.6 m) high and weigh 25 to 50 pounds (9–23 kilograms).

Coyotes mate in January through March. Most coyotes live alone or in pairs. Sometimes they form packs of three or more to help hunt for food in the fall or winter. They communicate by howls, yips, yelps, and whines.

ABOUT THE BOBCAT

Bobcats are North America's most common wildcat. They can survive in a variety of habitats, except in areas of extreme cold, because they have soft pads instead of fur on the bottoms of their paws. They are found from southern Canada to Mexico and live in deserts, forests, mountains, or swamps. In the Southwest, bobcats prefer brushy areas, canyons, and wooded mesas (broad, flat-topped hills with one or more clifflike sides). Most people never see bobcats in the wild because they avoid people.

These wildcats have keen senses of vision and hearing. They often quietly and slowly sneak up on their prey and catch it. They can leap and pounce from up to 10 feet (3 m) away on an animal, killing their meal immediately. Bobcats hunt for food at twilight and throughout the night. They eat mostly rabbits, but also feed on rodents, squirrels, porcupines, and sometimes young deer. They go after game birds such as wild turkeys, quails, pheasants, waterfowl, and farm chickens and geese. Usually bobcats look for prey on the ground, although they sometimes hunt while climbing in trees.

The bobcat has a short, black-tipped tail of 4 to 7 inches (10–18 cm) long. About twice the size of an average pet cat, the head and body of an adult bobcat usually measures 26 to 41 inches (66–104 cm) long. Males weigh 20 to 30 pounds (9–14 kg). Females are smaller, weighing 11 to 20 pounds (5–9 kg).

The bobcat's fur is brown or brownish red with a white underbelly.

Bobcats are solitary. They mate in late winter or early spring. To raise their young, females make and live in dens under logs, in thickets, or in hollow trees.

ABOUT THE PRAIRIE DOG

Prairie dogs are social, burrowing rodents that live on prairies and open grasslands of the western United States. These plump animals have light brown fur, a short tail and legs, small ears, and sharp front claws that they use to dig tunnels. About the size of a football, adults measure 9 to 15 inches (23–38 cm) long, including the tail, and weigh 1 to 3 pounds (0.5–1.4 kg). They have keen eyesight and a distinct vocal communication system.

Five types of prairie dogs live in the United States. The most common types are the black-footed and the white-footed prairie dog. Prairie dogs live in large, tightly knit groups called towns or villages. Prairie dogs burrow deep into the ground to make rooms connected by tunnels of up to 50 feet (15 m) long. The tunnel entrances are ringed by piles of soil. A town may contain hundreds of prairie dogs and typically covers less than half a square mile (1.3 square kilometers). If towns are in a farmer's or rancher's pasture, the many animals eat the grasses that cattle and horses eat, leaving less food for livestock. Prairie dogs may also ruin hay, wheat, alfalfa, or corn crops.

Prairie dogs sleep at night. During the day, they feed on grasses, roots, and seeds. To warn of predators, some prairie dogs stand guard on the mounds at tunnel entrances. When predators approach, the guards give warning barks or yips and

Prairie dog burrows have certain areas for nurseries, sleeping, and toilets. They also have listening posts located near exits.

bob up and down, then call again. The guards and animals aboveground then rush into the burrows. Prairie dogs can run up to 35 miles per hour (60 km/h) for short distances. When the danger has passed, the guards sound an all-clear call.

During the winter, prairie dogs stay underground and hibernate (they are dormant, or inactive, during cold months). Black-tailed prairie dogs mate in late January. The mating season for white-tailed prairie dogs is from March to April.

ABOUT THE RACCOON

Raccoons have a ringed, bushy tail and a band of black fur around the eyes. The black fur looks like a mask. Their long fur is typically gray. Raccoons measure 24 to 42 inches (61 to 107 centimeters) in length, including their tail. Most weigh 8 to 20 pounds (3.6–9 kg). Raccoons are found throughout most of the United States and southern Canada. They prefer streams, rivers, lakes, woods, and swamps but have adapted to other environments.

One reason raccoons are so widely found is that their fast, nimble front paws grab and handle all kinds of food. For instance, they pluck frogs, crayfish, clams, fish, and snails out of water. Another reason they are adaptable is that they eat nearly anything. In addition to water creatures, raccoons feed on slugs, insects, carrion (rotting, dead animals), vegetables, fruits, nuts, and seeds. Sometimes they hunt young mice, rats, squirrels, and gophers. They will even open people's garbage cans and eat the garbage.

Raccoons live both on the ground and in trees. They are nocturnal animals, so they hunt for food at night and sleep and raise their young in dens during the day. Den sites include abandoned burrows, openings in rock piles, deserted buildings, fallen trees, and tree holes. Raccoons move to different dens fre-

Homeowners have tried various remedies to keep raccoons out of their garbage, including hanging blinking Christmas lights around trash cans and sprinkling ammonia on garbage bags.

quently but randomly. They live alone or in small family groups. Their mating season is from January to June, peaking from March to April.

The intelligent raccoon is a fierce fighter when it is cornered. It has a keen sense of hearing and good eyesight. Excellent swimmers, raccoons are equally adept on land and can run up to 15 miles per hour (24 km/h).

ABOUT THE OPOSSUM

The opossum is the only marsupial (mammal with a pouch) native to North America. The female carries her babies inside her pouch for two months. The opossum lives in the eastern United States and as far west as Texas. There are also popu-

PLAYING DEAD

When threatened, an opossum might climb a tree to get away. It will growl, hiss, and bare its fifty razor-sharp teeth to scare off a predator. Otherwise, it works its jaw so that drool drips out of its mouth and bubbles come out of its nose. Then the predator will think the opossum is sick and will not try to catch it to eat it. If escape is impossible and the animal becomes very stressed, it goes into shock and looks as though it has died from an illness. The opossum falls on its side, curls its body, opens its mouth, sticks out its tongue, and goes limp. It drools and poops smelly, green diarrhea. The predator leaves the opossum alone and goes away. When the opossum thinks the danger has passed, it wiggles its ears to listen and raises its head to look around. If the environment is safe, it leaves. If danger remains, it plays dead again.

lations along the West Coast. Hunters often find them in wet areas, especially streams and swamps.

Opossums are solitary and nocturnal. They eat most kinds of plants, including grass, nuts, and fruit. They also hunt for mice,

According to *National Geographic*, opossums are not the only animals that play dead. So do leaf-litter frogs, fire-bellied toads, and hognose snakes.

insects, worms, snakes, birds, and eggs. In just minutes, one opossum can destroy a nest of game birds such as quail or break into a chicken coop and devour eggs. Sometimes opossums raid garbage cans and dumpsters.

Opossums nest in tree holes or in dens made by other animals. Their sharp claws and long, gripping tail help them climb trees swiftly. About the size of a pet cat, they measure 2.5 feet (76 cm) from nose to tail and weigh 9 to 13 pounds (4–6 kg). They have grayish-white fur, a long snout (nose, mouth, and jaw), pink nose, dark eyes, and large ears. Opossums usually mate in January through July.

To learn more about raccoons, opossums, coyotes, bobcats, or prairie dogs, hunters can visit zoos, read books, and watch videos. Experienced wildlife managers, hunters, local farmers, and ranchers are other good resources for researching these animals. In addition, hunters may want to watch and photograph the animals in the wild before hunting them.

CHAPTER THREE

HOW TO PREPARE

Varmints usually have a keen sense of smell and sharp hearing and vision. They can flee quickly and utilize camouflage to hide. To successfully hunt, you should carefully prepare so that you have stacked the odds in your favor as much as you can before you get out in the field. Such preparation includes handling and practicing with your weapons, scouting, and preparing other clothing and equipment.

GETTING THE PAPERWORK IN ORDER

The most important prerequisite for varmint hunting is to obtain and read the state and federal regulations that control the hunt. Hunters must know what gun or archery equipment can be used on specific types of wild animals. They must know where hunting is allowed, what days, what time of the day, and what hunting methods are allowed in their state and region. Hunting methods include the use of dogs or hunting at night. For instance, the prairie dog in most states is considered a nuisance and can be harvested year round using any method. In contrast, the regulations for hunting bobcats in the two neighboring states of Minnesota and Wisconsin are quite different. Local state departments of natural resources publish a hunting license book every year. This information is also found on these departments' websites.

Before going hunting, hunters must buy the proper hunting licenses or permits. Every state offers beginning and adult hunter education programs. A hunter's successful completion of this course leads to a certificate of graduation. The age when young hunters can begin to hunt alone often depends on when they have earned their safety certificate.

In addition to state training programs, hunters can gain valuable knowledge about varmints, predators, and hunting from

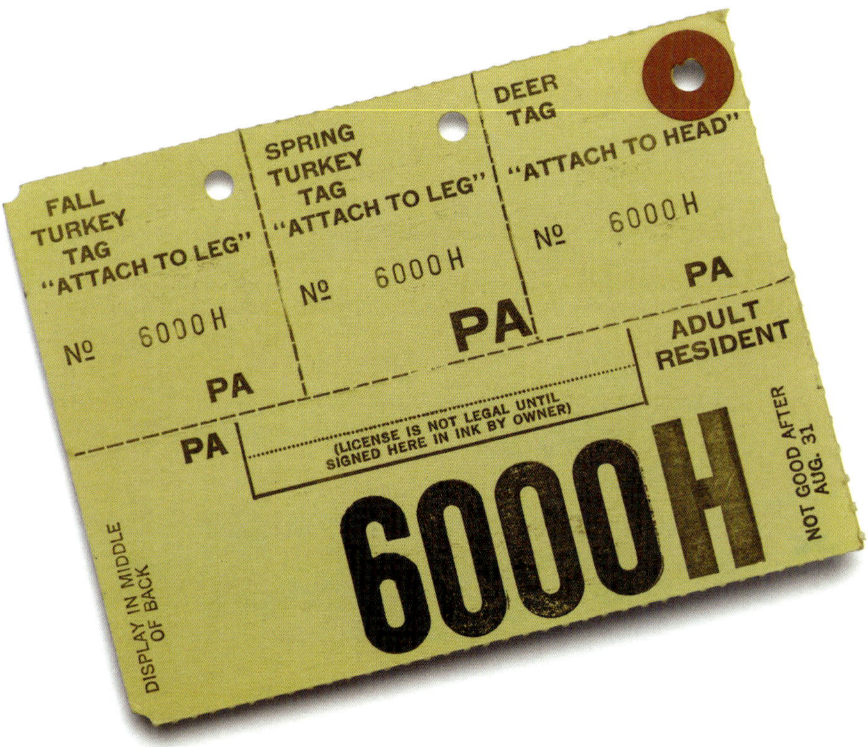

Hunting licenses date back to Colonial times in America, where they were often used to keep nonresidents from hunting certain animals.

gun clubs, sporting clubs, and farm and ranch organizations such as 4H and Future Farmers of America. Local hunters who are experienced with varmint hunting are often available to help beginning hunters. Rifle, shotgun, and archery clubs are common throughout the United States and Canada. They provide access to hunting preparation information, tips, and methods.

ACCESSING PRIVATE LAND AND SCOUTING

Gaining access to the particular varmint being hunted is important. It is critical that varmint habitat and access to that varmint are found well in advance of the actual hunt. People use county maps, which identify land ownership, and topographic and aerial maps. All these maps are usually available free online. Local state departments of natural resources, farm and ranch organizations, and local sporting clubs can lead beginning hunters to geographic areas and then to specific land parcels where varmint populations exist. Farmers and ranchers are usually enthusiastic about having hunters reduce a varmint population on their property.

Varmint hunting is often a way to reduce or control a population of nuisance animal in a specific area. Every state has professional wildlife managers who can direct varmint hunters to the targeted animal's range. When an area has been determined to have a potentially high number of varmints, and the hunters have gained permission to hunt on private land, then scouting is a wise next step when preparing to hunt. Scouting to determine the best place to hunt is as important as the actual hunt. When scouting, hunters spend time walking, looking, and judging the land. They walk the property by daylight, taking note of bush areas or clearings, and dangerous areas like cliffs, ditches, and

While GPS devices are commonly used by hunters, if the batteries die or the device malfunctions, it can be useful to have a compass along with a topo map to find your location.

rivers. They also look for some physical landmarks so they know which way to head out when they are finished.

Digital and automatic still cameras and camcorders (video cameras) are common tools when scouting a region because they allow hunters to photograph the animals living there. While walking, a Global Positioning System (GPS) device can be used to clearly and accurately mark future hunting sites on a map. Writing notes in a journal that is dedicated to future varmint hunting sites is another technique that can enhance successful hunts.

SHARP SHOOTING

Savvy varmint hunters select small caliber, fast speed, and low trajectory (flight path) ammunition. However, a .22 long rifle caliber, 20-gauge shotgun, or 30-pound bow is adequate to hunt raccoons, opossums, or bobcats. Larger weight and faster bullets, such as the .243 or 6mm Remington, are required to harvest large predators, such as the coyote, or long-range varmints, like the prairie dog. The key for success with any rifle, gun, or bow is sharp shooting, or the ability to hit a small target. Sharp shooting is a skill that demands many hours of patient, concentrated practice. Hunters must know exactly how their gun operates, fires, and feels before shooting at a varmint.

The skill to shoot straight develops over time by taking many practice shots. Shooting from a solid rest or bench at a stationary target at different distances will greatly improve a hunter's ability to harvest varmints. Shooters should practice with targets or at private shooting ranges. In many areas, shooting ranges that charge a fee are available for practice.

WHAT TO WEAR

After scouting, a varmint hunter needs clothing that is matched to the hunting area. If the site contains swampy soil or mountainous or hilly land, hunters should have sturdy leather and rubber boots. Rain gear and waders may be necessary, too. Warm clothing is a must when hunters plan to sit for hours in the cold or snow. A camou-

Hunting dogs are valuable companions. Be sure they are properly trained and equipped to keep them safe.

flage parka with a flap-up hood is excellent outerwear when cold weather or strong winds are predicted on the day of the hunt.

Varmint hunters must be equipped properly for their personal safety and the safety of their dogs, particularly when they are hunting at night. Good hunting lights and extra batteries are essential for hunters to find their way through woods. Some hunting lights, such as those used for hunting raccoons, fit onto special hardhats. The battery cable runs down one side of the hat to the waist and attaches to a battery pack that is placed in a pocket. Hunters adjust the brightness of the beam with a control knob. Night hunters can also use fabric caps that are fitted with mounting brackets on the visor to hold headlights. Hunters can choose belt clips for their lights or use headband headlights. Some raccoon hunters fit amber or red plastic lenses over their hunting lights. Animals notice colored light less than white light.

Hunters may use dogs when they are hunting some

CAMOUFLAGING YOURSELF

Because varmints have excellent vision, hunters wear clothing that blends into whatever color the land and plants are at the location and season of the hunt. Camouflage clothing might be all white in snow, patchy green in dark green tree foliage, or dusky tan on open grasslands and prairies. Camouflage clothing includes gloves, hats, jackets, pants, and boots. Varmint hunters who are after predators like the coyote and bobcat may use face paint or a headnet because these animals need to be called in close to harvest them. Many shooters cover the shiny parts on their guns, scopes, and bow with camouflage tape or dull spray paint. Raccoons and coyotes have excellent hearing. When hunting these varmints, hunters find that wearing clothing made from quiet material is important. Popular choices of materials are polar fleece, wool, a well-washed polyester-cotton blend, or other fabric that has a low nap (a soft or fuzzy surface).

varmints. If they do so, they need to keep track of them as they chase through the woods after the varmints. Dog collars equipped with lights are a good idea. Many hunters have tracking devices on their dogs' collars, which help them find lost or injured dogs. Varmints typically run swiftly when chased. The varmint and chasing dogs may travel so quickly that hunters lose track of them all. A tracking device helps hunters find their dogs. Practicing with dogs at night before going on an actual hunt leads to hunting success and reduces the chance of the loss of a dog.

CHAPTER FOUR

ON THE HUNT

Each hunter needs to adjust methods and strategies depending on a number of factors, including the varmint's specific habitat, the season, and the local terrain. Pursuit of small, quick-witted animals can be challenging for your mind and body—and those of your companions and dogs. These tips will give you a leg up on the most important part of your hunting endeavors.

HUNTING COYOTES

Hunters usually focus on three methods when hunting coyotes. One way is to call coyotes to the hunter by making the sound of a wounded rabbit. Another technique is to bring the animals to a hunter by baiting them with meat. Hunters can also stalk this varmint on foot.

Calling a coyote with a mouth-blown commercial call or with an electronic player is effective during all months of the year. The call imitates the cry of a wounded or dying rabbit, the favorite food of coyotes. Although used any time of the day, calling works best at sunrise or sunset when coyotes are actively hunting. Before calling, hunters conceal themselves in blinds,

While some hunters may want to buy devices to mimic animal calls, others use apps on their smartphones for this purpose.

or they wear camouflage clothing and remain still. They must be ready to make a fast shot at a swift target because coyotes within the hearing area approach the calling position quickly. To start, professionals recommend sitting quietly for ten to fifteen minutes, then calling loudly. Slowly tapering off the dying rabbit sound makes the call more realistic. Calling should get louder as the night goes on to bring coyotes in from farther away. If no coyotes appear within an hour, the hunter should move to another location.

Coyote baiting is a customary hunting method. Hunters place bait (food) regularly in an area known to host a coyote population. The bait often is a dead deer or another roadkill animal. The local game warden may need to issue a permit for possession of a road-killed carcass (dead animal). Other bait includes offal (guts) from local farmers or ranchers or scraps of meat purchased from grocery or meat stores. The meat attracts birds of prey, such as eagles, magpies, crows, and vultures. In turn, the noisy calling of these birds attracts coyotes.

To bait effectively, hunters must be scent free and wear clean clothes. They should hide within camouflage, such as a pit dug into the ground, a tree stand, or a ground blind. Hiding inside a brush pile also works well. Shots at feeding coyotes are usually taken at long range. Hunters use fast velocity, low trajectory (flight path), small-grain caliber rifles like the .22/250 or .25/06 Remington. When hunting varmints, serious big game hunters often use large-caliber, such as .270 or .30-06, rifles loaded with lightweight bullets. Hunters can set up automatic cameras to scout the time of day and number of feeding coyotes.

The third strategy to harvest coyotes requires snow. Two or more hunters drive along on country roads in the winter and look for fresh coyote tracks. Once fresh spoor is located, one hunter is stationed in an area ahead of the coyote's direc-

CONCEALING YOURSELF

Hunters need to make sure that coyotes cannot smell them. Coyotes are wild members of the dog family. All dogs have a keen sense of smell and can easily detect a human in their area. Any human or unusual scent alerts the coyote to an intruder. Hunters must control odor from perspiration, urination, and so on. Sometimes hunters must relieve themselves in the woods. They should dig a hole, relieve themselves, and then bury their waste and any used toilet paper. Human odor is minimized by hunting downwind of coyotes and keeping all clothing clean and free of human scent. Using soap and laundry detergent without a scent is recommended for washing clothing. Sporting goods stores sell scent-free laundry soaps. Hunting equipment should not smell like cleaning oil and cleaning solvents during the actual hunt.

tion of travel. The other hunter returns to the fresh tracks and then slowly walks or stalks the coyote. This hunting style requires good binoculars to scan the area ahead for signs of the coyote. If successful, the tracking hunter flushes the coyote past the second posted hunter. Otherwise, the tracker might sneak up on a feeding or sleeping coyote. Wind direction is important because a coyote's sense of smell is very good. Hunters use a compass or GPS to know their position. Cell phones are useful, where legal, for the team of hunters to communicate a coyote's unpredictable escape path during the hunt.

HUNTING BOBCATS

Bobcat-hunting methods depend on the hunting area and time of year. The most common and successful strategy for hunting the bobcat is by calling. Like coyotes, bobcats are called by the sound of a dying or wounded rabbit. The shrill, wailing sound carries long distances and a bobcat within hearing distance moves into the area. The call imitates the distress and dying sound of a rabbit, which is easy prey for a bobcat. Hunters can make this presentation even more attractive by hanging a thin, dark strip of cloth or a dark feather from a low branch. The moving cloth or feather draws the bobcat's attention to the snowy white background and away from the hunter.

To harvest a bobcat, hunters use a small-caliber rifle identical to the kind used for coyote hunting. Nonexpanding bullets

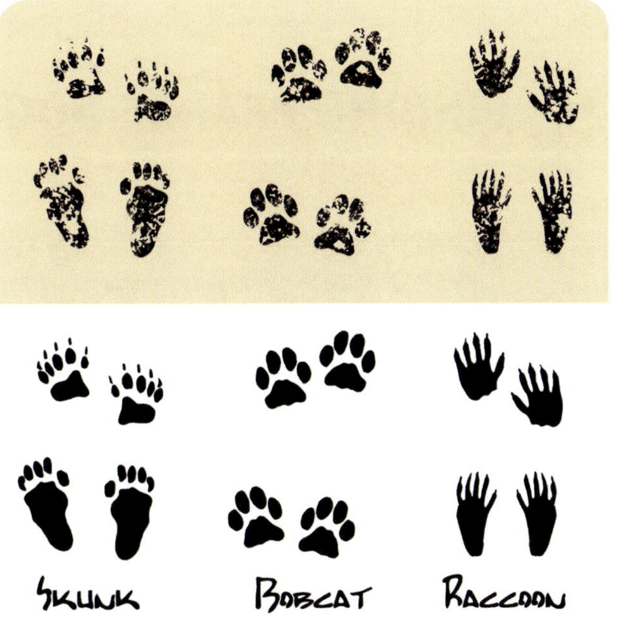

Courses in animal-track identification can increase your awareness of the outdoors as well as help you determine which animals left which tracks.

are critical so as not to damage the pelt (fur). During calling, bobcat hunters should wear full camouflage, such as all-white clothing in the winter if there is snow or regular camouflage clothing when no snow is present. They must remain quiet and motionless until the animal comes within shooting range.

In some states, bobcat hunting with dogs, such as foxhounds, is permissible. Using dogs requires the hunters to find bobcat tracks that are crossing a road or trail and then releasing the hounds to follow the fresh spoor. Eventually, the wildcat tires and climbs a tree or turns to fight the dogs while it is at bay. The hunters follow behind the howling dogs and harvest the bobcat. While the bobcat is treed, the shot is at close range, so hunters use small-caliber rifles or archery.

FINDING PRAIRIE DOGS

To hunt prairie dogs, hunters must find a village of animals on an accessible prairie. Many ranchers seek out and appreciate shooters who will reduce or eliminate a local population. Active during the day, prairie dogs quickly retreat to their underground burrows when they are threatened. Hunters need to be concerned about the animal's excellent vision. This characteristic can be overcome by long-distance shooting.

Typically, hunters set up firm benches or tripods for stability, which allow accurate shooting up to 200 to 300 yards (183–274 m) at these small targets. They need a clear line of sight and a sturdy backstop, such as a hill, in the direction they will be shooting. Small-grain fast-caliber rifles with scopes are used because of the long distance of the targets. Scope magnification is typically 5x10 power. Some varmint hunters prefer 20 power.

Most serious prairie dog hunters use high-magnification scopes on tripods to visually scan the prairie. When prairie dogs are located, the shooters switch to rifles. Two or three rifles per hunter are needed because fast, constant shooting makes the rifle barrel red hot and destroys the accuracy. Other essential equipment for hunting prairie dogs includes good binoculars, shaded shooting glasses, and a brimmed hat.

PURSUING RACCOONS AND OPOSSUMS

Raccoons and opossums are active at night, making it difficult or impossible to hunt them during the day. The method that consistently results in a good harvest is hunting with coon dogs. Dog breeds that hunt by scent include the Walker, bluetick, redtick, redbone, black-and-tan, and English coon dog. These dogs track and follow fresh varmint scents. Raccoon and opossum hunting are usually done in small groups. The chase begins when two to four hunters release several coon dogs on a spoor, or fresh track. Because the tracking is done at night, hunters need to be aware of the land, water, and other road and area characteristics. The coon dogs chase and follow the fresh scent of a raccoon or opossum until the animal climbs a tree. The dogs circle the tree and continue to bark wildly. Meanwhile, the hunters follow the sound of the barking dogs.

Once at the site, hunters shoot the treed animal at close range, usually with a small-caliber rifle such as the .22 long rifle hollow point. Night hunters carry their rifles cased during the hunt and uncase them to take the actual shot to harvest the raccoon or opossum. For safety, one hunter is designated as the shooter. Loaded guns at night are dangerous because it is difficult to know exactly where the muzzle is aimed. Shotguns can be

This hunter is helping his son shoot a .22-caliber rifle from a distance. It's a good idea to get help in the field when you are a beginning hunter.

used. However, at close range, the valuable hide and meat are ruined. Some hunters prefer archery equipment. They need to be careful while they are tracking and running through the woods because the bow and arrows could break as they hit unseen trees in the black of night.

Many night varmint hunters use a GPS tracking device to determine their exact location. Strong headlamps or flashlights are necessary for hunters to safely walk through the woods and to see while shooting a treed varmint. Wise hunters always carry spare batteries.

CHAPTER FIVE

AFTER THE HARVEST

Responsible, effective, seasoned hunters know how important it is to properly care for their quarry immediately after they have harvested it. Following the hunt, it is imperative to immediately see to the meat and hide. Careful attention to weapons and other hunting equipment must also be dealt with. Finally, evaluate what went right and what went wrong in order to improve during the next hunt.

HOW TO USE THE MEAT

A varmint requires attention immediately after the harvest. To make certain the meat is tasty and safe, hunters must cool the carcass as soon as possible. If the weather is 40 degrees Fahrenheit (4 degrees Celsius) or below, taking the internal organs from the body cavity allows the carcass to cool quickly. If the hunting is done during warm weather, gutting the animal and putting the carcass on ice or in a cooler as soon as practical is mandatory for obtaining quality meat and hides.

Raccoon, opossum, and even prairie dogs have edible, savory meat if cooled quickly. The meat needs to be butchered

Harvested meat is often allowed to hang in order to make for tender, delicious, high-quality meals.

and sliced into small portions and cleaned in cold water. The meat is then ready for cooking. For future use, the meat is packaged, labeled, and frozen.

Meat that is cooled quickly, cleaned, and properly cared for is a source of pride to many hunters. Good hunters host and share their rewards often with family and friends. A variety of resources, including books, magazines, and websites, are devoted to wild game meat, including the butchering, care, and preparation of the animals for eating. People enjoy raccoon and opossum meat in stews, chilies, and soups. They can slow cook, grill, fry, barbecue, roast, or smoke the meat.

CARING FOR HIDES

The raccoon, coyote, and bobcat are valuable furbearers. When properly cared for, their plush, thick hide is valuable for clothing. People who live in northern latitudes in Canada, Russia, and northern China use wild animal hides to make warm, winter clothing.

Hunters must care for the fur of their harvested animal to ensure that it is usable. They must give special attention so as not to damage the hair because of rough handling, such as pulling the animal through brush, swamps, or grass. Many varmint hunters strip or skin the hide from the carcass while they are still in the woods. They can then place several hides into a packsack for carrying through the woods. Because people do not eat coyote and bobcat meat, skinning the collected animals in the woods and leaving the carcass for other predators to eat solves two problems at once. The valuable fur hide is protected from hair damage, and the carcass and offal provide an easy meal for other wildlife. Birds and wild mammals of all types feed heavily on carcass meat and bones left to rot in the woods after harvests.

Eagles, buzzards, and crows feast on carrion, and small rodents chew up the bones for calcium, a necessary nutrient for bones and teeth.

Removing the hide of all varmints is accomplished using the same basic method. Hunters hang the animal by both hind legs and cut the hide completely around each hind foot. They make an incision (cut) on the underside of each leg down from the foot to the vent (anus). Then they pull the hide down and off the carcass, similar to pulling off a glove. Next, hunters carefully cut around the ears, eyes, and nose and pull the hide completely free of the carcass. A small, sharp knife is the only tool required to skin a hide. Books and videos are available that show the hide removal and meat butchering methods used for varmints.

If hunters do not want to prepare their hides, they can take their animals to professional fur buyers who will skin the hides and purchase them from the hunters. Fur buyers can be found throughout the United States. This transaction is common with coyotes, raccoons, and bobcats. Opossum and prairie dog hides are not commercially used. Hunters discard these hides with the offal and carcass.

Most varmint hunters seek their targeted wild animals on private land. It is essential and common courtesy for hunters to thank the landowner after a hunt. Private land owners always enjoy some gesture of appreciation such as an offering of meat, a thank-you card, or volunteer work on their property or with their livestock. The next hunt depends on access to the land on which the varmint lives. Experienced hunters do not take for granted permission to access private land. In addition to helping ranchers and farmers control nuisance pests, many varmint hunters and landowners become long-term friends.

While there are different methods for tanning hides, most of them involve scraping the meat off and soaking the pelts in salt solutions.

REMEMBERING THE HUNT

Varmint hunting is enhanced in both successful harvests and enjoyable memories by documenting the hunt. Digital photographs and videos of the wild animals and the hunt give much satisfaction and pleasure during the off-season. Hunters should write a journal entry after every hunt. Journaling can be done on paper or electronically. Capturing the essentials of who, what, when, where, and how from each outdoor attempt to hunt varmints provides a basis for future hunts. The temperature, wind direction, and storm fronts should also be documented along with details of the hunt. The journal should include maps of the area that was hunted. Most state departments of natural resources provide free topographical maps. Aerial maps are free on websites such as Google Earth (http://earth.google.com).

Successful varmint harvests are based on the skill, ability, and experience of a hunter. This requires memory of precise details of the hunt that allowed success or resulted in failure. The time spent hunting varmints is usually limited by other important activities, such as school, time with family and friends, work, or other obligations. When the opportunity to hunt arises, having details of previous outdoor varmint-shooting experiences gives hunters a better chance to score a hit on the targeted varmint.

KEEPING EQUIPMENT IN ORDER

Once the meat and hide are cared for, savvy hunters focus on their equipment and the clothing that was used in the hunt. This should be taken care of whether or not the hunt was successful. Hunters dry, clean, and oil their guns, scopes, and archery equipment. They look for any breaks or damaged parts that need

USEFUL DEVICES

Various technologies give hunters an easy, quick, and reliable way to make advanced preparations based on the details of past hunts. Some digital cameras have GPS devices as part of the memory so that when a photo is taken, the exact location (latitude and longitude) is printed on the photo. This location can be downloaded onto topographical or aerial maps when the hunter has returned home. It is easy for the varmint hunter to keep maps at home or carry them into the woods with locations marked for placing blinds, calling in varmints, locating prairie dog villages, or identifying dangerous landforms, such as cliffs with steep drop-offs. The locations of varmint dens, feeding areas, or regularly followed game trails can be mapped and plotted on topographic or aerial maps. Whether using a handheld GPS, a camera with built-in GPS, or memory, the marking of maps helps the hunter efficiently select excellent scoping, calling, or hunting sites for future hunts.

repair. Because prairie dog shooters may have fired hundreds of rounds of ammunition, they need to give their rifle bore special attention. Rifle shooters thoroughly scrub the barrel's bore with solvent and brass brushes until the copper and lead deposits are removed. Then applying a final light oil coating protects the steel bore from rusting. Hunters who clean and check their equipment are well prepared to hunt again. Experienced hunters have safe, dependable, and established areas in their garages or homes where all hunting equipment is stored

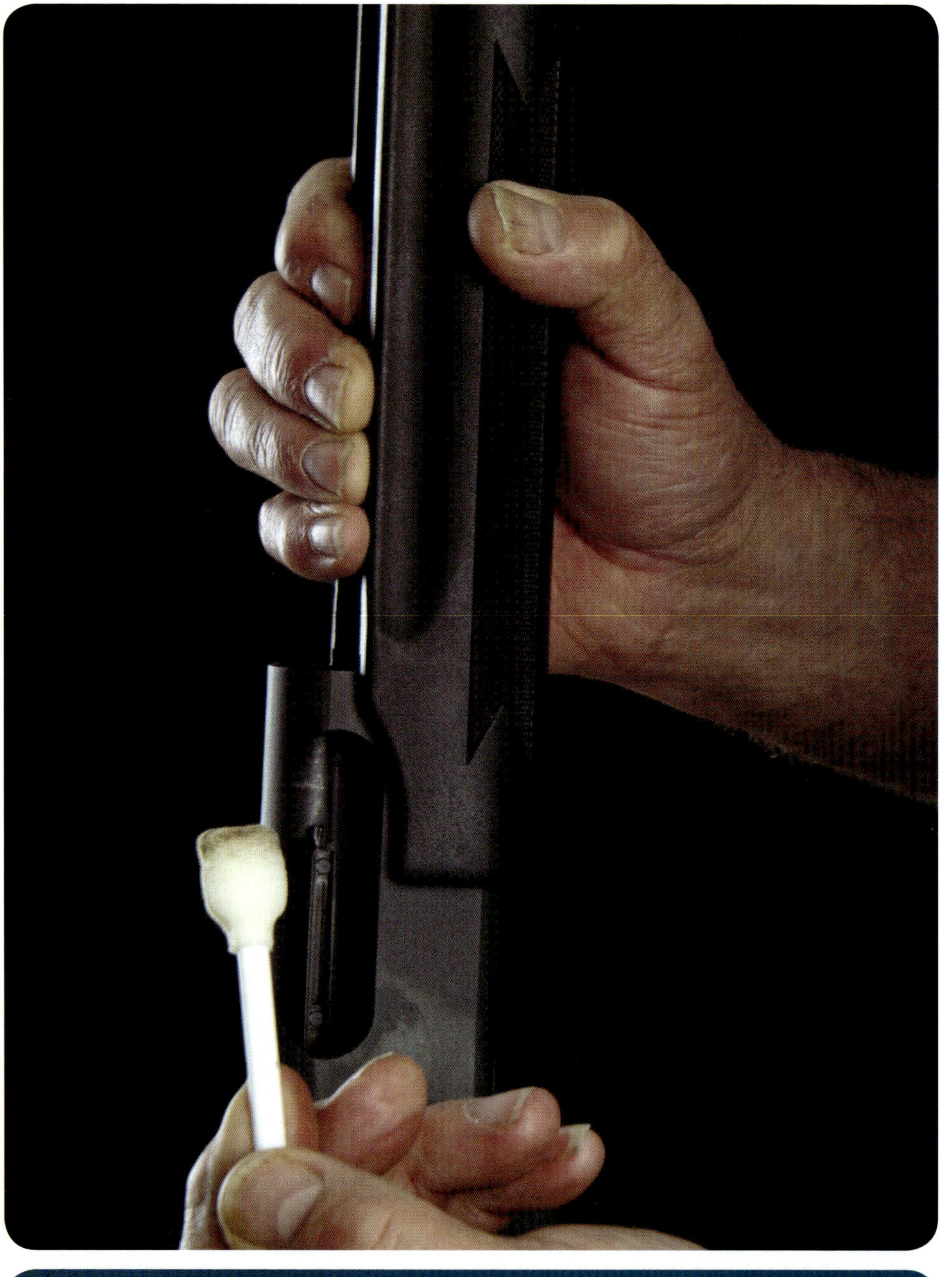

It is essential to clean your weapon after it has been fired. Any debris in the chamber will negatively affect the weapon's accuracy.

for safety and fast retrieval when the next hunt arrives. Gun owners are strongly encouraged to store all rifles, shotguns, and pistols in a secured metal safe.

Varmint hunters often use some electronic equipment. They may have headlamps, flashlights, calling devices, GPS devices, range finders, pocket digital cameras, and camcorders. When hunting in groups, two-way radios are often used. Hunters need to remove the batteries from all electronic devices then clean and store the equipment. Having an organized storage area for equipment allows hunters to be efficient when preparing and planning the next hunt. Varmint hunting gives a hunter the pride of knowing that the landowner has benefited from the hunt by reducing or eliminating a pesky varmint population. The hunt also benefits the hunter if he or she can become friends with the landowner, which may lead to private land access during big or small game hunting, too.

GLOSSARY

ammunition Bullets and gunpowder used in firearms.

archery The skill of shooting with a bow and arrow.

bag limit The number of a particular type of animal that a hunter can harvest during a day.

barrel The metal tube of a rifle.

blind A shelter, often camouflaged, used for concealing hunters.

bore The hollow part inside a gun barrel.

butcher To process an animal's meat into usable sizes.

caliber The inside diameter of the barrel of a rifle or the diameter of a bullet.

camouflage Anything that conceals a person or equipment by appearing to be part of the natural surroundings.

carrion Rotting, dead animals.

flush To cause a hidden animal to move out of hiding suddenly.

furbearer An animal whose skin is covered with fur, especially fur that is commercially valuable.

game Wild animals hunted for food or sport.

Global Positioning System (GPS) Handheld computers that can calculate an exact position using a global positioning satellite.

habitat The area or environment where an animal lives.

harvest The act of shooting and recovering an animal.

illegal Against the law.

nocturnal Most active at night.

poacher A person who takes game in a forbidden area or game that is illegal to take.

possession limit The maximum number of a type of animal that can be in a hunter's possession at any time.

predator An animal that eats another living animal.

prerequisite A thing that is required as a prior condition for something else to happen or exist.

prey An animal hunted or caught for food.
scope A small telescope on a rifle barrel.
season The length of time to hunt specific game.
spoor The track or trail of an animal, especially a wild animal.
target Something that is aimed at to shoot with firearms or bow and arrow.
trespass To unlawfully enter a person's property.

FOR MORE INFORMATION

Canadian Parks and Wilderness Society
506-250 City Centre Avenue
Ottawa, ON K1R 6K7
Canada
(800) 333-9453
Website: http://www.cpaws.org
Facebook/Twitter: @cpaws
Instagram: @cpaws_national
A nationwide Canadian charity dedicated to protecting public land, water, and wildlife. It has aided in the protection of more than half a million square kilometres in over fifty years.

Canadian Shooting Sports Association (CSSA)
1143 Wentworth Street West, Unit 204
Oshawa, ON L1J 8P7
Canada
(888) 873-4339
Website: http://www.cdnshootingsports.org
Facebook: @cdnshootingsports
The CSSA supports and promotes all kinds of shooting sports, including hunting and archery, and works politically to fight for the rights of responsible Canadians to have unrestricted, lawful access to firearms.

International Hunter Education Association (IHEA)
800 East 73rd Avenue, Unit 2
Denver, CO 80229
(303) 430-7233
Website: http://www.ihea-usa.org
Facebook: @InternationalHunterEducationAssociation

IHEA's mission is "to continue the heritage of hunting worldwide by developing safe, responsible, knowledgeable and involved hunters."

National Bowhunter Education Foundation
PO Box 2934
Rapid City, SD 57709
(605) 716-0596
Website: http://www.nbef.org
This organization provides bowhunting education and classes across the United States, including the National Archery in the Schools Program (NASP).

National Rifle Association of America (NRA)
11250 Waples Mill Road
Fairfax, VA 22030
(800) 672-3888
Website: https://firearmtraining.nra.org
Facebook/Instagram: @NationalRifleAssociation
Twitter: @NRA
The NRA's training and education department offers a number of programs across the United States designed to teach shooters safe, ethical, and responsible firearm practices.

National Shooting Sports Foundation (NSSF)
Flintlock Ridge Office Center
11 Mile Hill Road
Newtown, CT 06470-2359
(203) 426-1320
Website: http://www.nssf.org
Facebook: @nssfcomm
Twitter: @NSSF
Instagram: @thenssf

The National Shooting Sports Foundation (NSSF) is the trade association for the shooting, hunting, and firearms industry. Formed in 1961, NSSF is a nonprofit organization that promotes, protects, and preserves hunting and the shooting sports.

National Wildlife Federation
11100 Wildlife Center Drive
Reston, VA 20190-5362
(800) 822-9919
Website: http://www.nwf.org
Facebook/Instagram: @nationalwildlife
Twitter: @nwf
Founded in 1936, the National Wildlife Federation works to protect and restore wildlife habitat.

U.S. Fish & Wildlife Service
1849 C Street NW
Washington, DC 20240
(800) 344-9453
Website: http://www.fws.gov
Facebook, Twitter, and Instagram: @usfws
This government agency manages the United States' natural resources in order to conserve, protect, and enhance wildlife, plants, and their habitats.

USDA Forest Service
Attn: Office of Communication
Mailstop: 1111
1400 Independence Avenue SW
Washington, DC 20250-1111
(800) 832-1355
Website: http://www.fs.fed.us

Facebook: @USForestService
Twitter: @forestservice
Instagram: @u.s.forestservice
An agency of the US Department of Agriculture, the Forest Service manages and maintains millions of acres of public lands in national forests and grasslands.

Sportsmen's Alliance
801 Kingsmill Parkway
Columbus, OH 43229
(614) 888-4868
Website: http://www.sportsmensalliance.org
Facebook: @sportsmensalliance
Twitter: @sportsmensall
The US Sportsmen's Alliance works to protect and advance the rights of hunters and scientific wildlife management professionals.

FOR FURTHER READING

Gaspar, Joe, and Jack Weaver. *Hunting*. New York, NY: Rosen Publishing, 2016.

Gish, Melissa. *Raccoons*. Mankato, MN: Creative Education/Creative Paperbacks, 2016.

Gurtler, Janet. *Small Game*. New York, NY: AV2 by Weigl, 2016.

Hansen, Grace. *Coyotes*. Minneapolis, MN: Abdo Kids, 2016.

Hemstock, Annie. *Bow Hunting*. New York, NY: Rosen Publishing, 2015.

Hemstock, Annie. *Hunting Laws and Safety*. New York, NY: Rosen Publishing, 2015.

Kalman, Bobbie. *Invasive Animal Species*. New York, NY: Crabtree Publishing Company, 2016.

Meyer, Susan. *Hunting Dogs: Different Breeds and Special Purposes*. New York, NY: Rosen Publishing, 2013.

Milner, Robert. *Absolutely Positively Gundog Training: Positive Training for Your Retriever Gundog*. CreateSpace, 2015.

Niver, Heather Moore. *Opossums After Dark*. New York, NY: Enslow Publishing, 2016.

Ringstad, Arnold. *Bobcats*. Mankato, MN: Amicus High Interest, 2015.

BIBLIOGRAPHY

Blair, Gerry. *Predator Calling with Gerry Blair.* Iola, WI: Krause Publications, 2007.

Brakefield, Tom. *Small Game Hunting.* Philadelphia, PA: J. B. Lippincott Company, 1978.

Churchill, James. *Field Dressing Small Game and Fowl.* Harrisburg, PA: Stackpole Books, 1987.

Creative Publishing. *Dressing and Cooking Wild Game.* Chanhassen, MN: Creative Publishing, 2000.

Geer, Galen. *Meat on the Table: Modern Small-Game Hunting.* Boulder, CO: Paladin Press, 1985.

GunnersDen. "Bobcat Hunting." GunnersDen.com. Retrieved December 15, 2017. http://www.gunnersden.com/index.htm.shooting-hunting-bobcat.html.

GunnersDen. "Coyote Hunting." Retrieved December 15, 2017. http://www.gunnersden.com/index.htm.shooting-hunting-coyote.html.

GunnersDen. "Varmint/ Predator Hunting." Retrieved December 15, 2017. http://www.gunnersden.com/index.htm.hunting-varmint.html.

Harrington, Dan. (Avid hunter, Rice Lake, WI). In discussion with the author, March 2010.

Jones, Paul Anthony. "22 Brilliant Old Nicknames for Animals." Mental Floss, August 12, 2014. http://mentalfloss.com/article/58331/22-brilliant-old-nicknames-animals.

Kansas Department of Wildlife and Parks. "Virginia Opossum." Retrieved December 15, 2017. http://www.kdwp.state.ks.us/news/Hunting/Furharvesting/Furbearers/Virginia-Opossum.

Lawrence, H. Lea. *The Ultimate Guide to Small Game and Varmint Hunting: How to Hunt Squirrels, Rabbits, Hares, Woodchucks, Coyotes, Foxes and More.* Guilford, CT: The Lyons Press, 2002.

Maas, David R. *North American Game Animals.* Minnetonka, MN:

Cy Decosse, 1995.

National Geographic. "Prairie Dogs." https://www.nationalgeographic.com/animals/mammals/group/prairie-dogs.

National Park Service. "Avoiding Unintentional Poisoning." September 27, 2017. https://www.nps.gov/samo/learn/management/rodenticides.htm.

National Shooting Sports Foundation. "The Ethical Hunter." Pamphlet, 2006.

Outdoor Empire Publishing. *Minnesota Firearms Safety Hunter Education, Student Manual.* Seattle, WA: Outdoor Empire Publishing, 2001.

Owen, James. "The Living Dead: Animals That Pretend to Go Belly-Up." *National Geographic*, October 19, 2015. https://news.nationalgeographic.com/2015/10/151019-playing-dead-frog-possum-toad-animals-behavior-science.

Peterson, David H. (Hunter education instructor, Two Harbors, MN). In discussion with the author, March 2010.

Schneck, Marcus. *The North America Hunter's Handbook.* Philadelphia, PA: Running Press, 1991.

Watson, Steve. (Avid varmint hunter, Cambridge, MN). In discussion with the author, March 2010.

INDEX

ABOUT THE AUTHORS

Xina M. Uhl has written numerous educational books for young people, in addition to textbooks, teacher's guides, lessons, and assessment questions. She has tackled subjects including sports, history, biographies, technology, and health concerns. Although she has friends and family who hunt, she shoots animals only through her camera lens. Her blog details her publications as well as interesting facts and the occasional cat picture.

Judy Monroe Peterson is married to an avid hunter who has more than fifty years of hunting experience. She has earned two master's degrees and is the author of many educational books for young people. Currently, she is a writer and editor of K–12 and post–high school curriculum materials on a variety of subjects, including biology, life science, and the environment.

ABOUT THE CONSULTANT

Benjamin Cowan has over twenty years of both big game and small game hunting experience. In addition to being an avid hunter, Cowan is also a member of many conservation organizations. He currently resides in west Tennessee.

PHOTO CREDITS

Cover Westend61/Getty Images; back cover Drakuliren/Shutterstock.com; pp. 4–5 (background) Outdoor_Media/Shutterstock.com; p. 5 Academ/Shutterstock.com; p. 6 jadimages /Shutterstock.com; pp. 7, 17, 27, 35, 43 Jed Packer/Shutterstock.com; p. 8 Mandelbrot2 /Shutterstock.com; p. 9 Lee Rentz/Alamy Stock Photo; pp. 10–11 Steve Byland/Shutterstock .com; pp. 12–13 Henk Bentiage/Shutterstock.com; p. 18 Don Mammoser/Shutterstock.com; pp. 20–21 Evikka/Shutterstock.com; p. 23 Tom Middleton/Shutterstock.com; p. 25 Andrew Skolnick/Shutterstock.com; p. 28 Mega Pixel/Shutterstock.com; p. 30 NEStudio/Shutterstock .com; pp. 32–33 nesneJkraM/E+/Getty Images; p. 36 Mitch Kezar/Design Pics/Getty Images; p. 39 Natural_Warp/DigitalVision Vectors/Getty Images; p. 42 Robert C. Paulson/Alamy Stock Photo; p. 44 Clay Hunting/EyeEm/Getty Images; p. 47 AlessandraRC/Shutterstock.com; p. 50 Sheila Fitzgerald/Shutterstock.com.

Design: Michael Moy; Photo Research: Xina M. Uhl